Our Global Community

Schools

Lisa Easterling

www.heinemann.co.uk/library
Visit our website to find out more information about Heinemann Library books.

To order:
 Phone 44 (0) 1865 888066
 Send a fax to 44 (0) 1865 314091
 Visit the Heinemann Bookshop at www.heinemann.co.uk/library to browse our catalogue and order online.

First published in Great Britain by Heinemann Library, Halley Court, Jordan Hill, Oxford OX2 8EJ, part of Harcourt Education. Heinemann is a registered trademark of Harcourt Education Ltd.

Editorial: Diyan Leake
Design: Joanna Hinton-Malivoire
Picture research: Ruth Smith
Production: Duncan Gilbert

Origination: Chroma Graphics (Overseas) Pte Ltd
Printed and bound in China by South China
 Printing Company Ltd

ISBN 978 0 431 19120 1
11 10 09 08 07
10 9 8 7 6 5 4 3 2 1

British Library Cataloguing in Publication Data
Easterling, Lisa
 Schools. - (Our global community)
 1. Elementary schools - Juvenile literature
 I. Title
 372

Acknowledgements
The publishers would like to thank the following for permission to reproduce photographs: Alamy Images pp. **4** (Dan Atkin), **10** (Blend Images), **12** (Stock Connection Blue), **13** (Hornbil Images Pvt Ltd), **16** (Royal Geographical Society), **17** (Danita Delimont), **19** (Sue Cunningham Photographic); Corbis pp. **5** (Michael Prince), **6** (Michael Prince), **7**, **8** (Creasource), **11** (Anders Ryman), **14** (Dean Conger), **15** (Tomas Van Houtryve), **18** (Gideon Mendel), **20** (Gideon Mendel), **21** (Karen Kasmauski), **22** (Creasource), **23** (Michael Prince; Creasource); Getty Images p. **9** (Taxi).

Cover photograph of children at school in Yap, Federated States of Micronesia, reproduced with permission of Alamy/Photo Resource Hawaii.

Every effort has been made to contact copyright holders of any material reproduced in this book. Any omissions will be rectified in subsequent printings if notice is given to the publishers.

Contents

Schools around the world

All around the world, children go to school.

Children go to school to learn.

Teachers teach children.

Children learn to read and write.

board

Teachers write on boards.

book

Children read books.

Getting to school

Some children walk to school.

Some children ride bikes to school.

Some children go to school by bus.

Some children go to school by boat.

Types of schools

Some schools are in big cities.

Some schools are in the country.

Some schools are outside.

Some schools are in homes.

Some schools are only for girls.

Some schools are only for boys.

Working in schools

Sometimes children work alone
at school.

Sometimes children work together
at school.

School vocabulary

board

teacher

pupil

desk

Picture glossary

 **board** large board that a teacher writes on

 **teacher** person who teaches children

Index

Notes for parents and teachers

Before reading

Talk to the children about school. What do they like best about school? How do they travel to school?

After reading

School time. Use an analogue clock and talk through with the children what times different things happen in the school day; for example, "At nine o'clock we have assembly. Play time is at half past ten," and so on. Then move the clock hands and ask the children what they do at that time.

School song. Make up verses to sing to the tune of "The Farmer's in His Den"; for example, "We all come to school, we all come to school, E-I-addio, we all come to school." Other verses could be "We all go out to play", "We all have our lunch", "We all do our maths" and so on.

What we do at school. Give each child a piece of A5 paper. Ask the children to draw themselves doing their favourite school activity. Stick all the portraits on to a length of wallpaper and write the heading: "Things we do at school". Display the poster on the wall.